the EVERYDAY Eco-Warrior

110 EASY TIPS FOR A ZERO-WASTE LIFE

SRINI & SHUBHASHREE

hachette INDIA

First published in 2021 by Hachette India
(Registered name: Hachette Book Publishing India Pvt. Ltd)
An Hachette UK company
www.hachetteindia.com

1

Book illustrations by Shubhashree Sangameswaran

ISBN 978-93-91028-53-4

Hachette Book Publishing India Pvt. Ltd
4th & 5th Floors, Corporate Centre,
Plot No. 94, Sector 44, Gurugram 122003, India

Typeset in Futura PT 11/16.5
by R. Ajith Kumar, New Delhi

Printed and bound in India
by Manipal Technologies Limited, Manipal

MIX
Paper from
responsible sources
FSC™ C043100

the EVERYDAY Eco-Warrior

Srini Swaminathan is a Chennai-based consultant in the social development sector. Over the last seven years, he has adopted small but impactful measures in his daily life on the path to sustainable living in urban India and has regularly shared his journey via print and social media. He has been plogging (picking trash while running) since 2013 and has also launched volunteer-driven awareness initiatives like Spot Fix Chennai, which aims to clean up the city's trash filled spots.

Shubhashree is a Bengaluru-based visual artist and illustrator who, among other things, loves to write. She is currently educating herself on living a low-impact life, and as part of the Let's Talk Trash project, she has produced illustrated books for adults and children to get the conversation started about our waste footprint. When she isn't cooking, baking, eating or dreaming about a favourite meal, she is probably making an illustration of it.

ALSO BY THE SAME AUTHORS

(Im)Perfectly Zero Waste: A No-Nonsense Guide to Living Sustainably in India

'You cannot get through a single day without having an impact on the world around you. What you do makes a difference, and you have to decide what kind of difference you want to make.'

— DR JANE GOODALL

'We don't have to engage in grand, heroic actions to participate in the process of change. Small acts, when multiplied by millions of people, can transform the world.'

— HOWARD ZINN

There are 500 times more microplastics in the ocean than the number of stars in the galaxy.

Every year we generate 2 billion tonnes of trash globally, and we are running out of landfill space.

Global waste generation is expected to increase by 70 per cent to 3.4 billion tonnes by the year 2050.

You have probably read these statistics somewhere. Statements like these seem alarmist and scare-monger-y, but they are, unfortunately, true. The idea behind this book, though, is not to alarm. It can get overwhelming, this business of caring for the future of our planet and trying to live sustainably. At times, we even stop and wonder where to begin, and whether our actions will make a difference at all. How is refusing a straw going to affect big corporations who don't care two hoots about the planet? What will switching to an eco-friendly laundry detergent really achieve? We hear you. It seems terribly unfair to put the burden on the consumer when change needs to happen at a higher level. However, our belief is that we have to start somewhere, and our hope is that these small steps will ultimately lead to collective awareness. And that this will, in turn, influence those in power to act and make policy changes. We do what is within our locus of control and influence while fighting the big fight.

There are a thousand things we can do to generate a little less waste and be a little less of a burden on our planet. In this book, we've tried to focus on 110 such ideas that are simple but have the potential to make a substantial difference.

We'd recommend you flip through the book and pick a section that appeals to you. From there, select one or two tips that fit into your current lifestyle, and try to stick with those until they become habits. And then you can move on to another, and then another. This book isn't going to sit on your bookshelf judging you and pointing fingers at you if you slip up or don't implement every tip you've read. Life can be complicated as it is, and our aim is to make things simple for you. So read on, share the book, share the tips with people, and give it your best shot!

CONTENTS

1

FOOD, GROCERIES AND EATING OUT

1.

Start with the end in mind

Here's a rule of thumb: Whenever you need to make a choice when it comes to shopping, pause for a moment and ask yourself a couple of questions:

1. What is the journey this object has taken to reach me?
2. What will happen to this when I'm done with it? Will this rot, can this be recycled, can it be reused, can its life be extended?

These questions are a good way to start thinking a bit more deeply about the things we buy.

2.

Grocery shopping? Remember the bags!

We've all been there, done that – shopped for groceries on the way back from work, only to realize at the billing counter that we forgot to carry our reusable bags. And so, we get some polythene bags that will ultimately end up in the landfill and take decades to even begin decomposing. To avoid this, it's a good idea to keep bags handy in your vehicle, backpack or purse so there's always one within reach. Have a few bags right next to your door so you don't forget them when you step out. Most reusable bags can be folded several times into the size of a handkerchief – those are particularly handy! Just remember to put the bags back in place once you're done emptying them after shopping.

3.

Reusable cutlery is cool

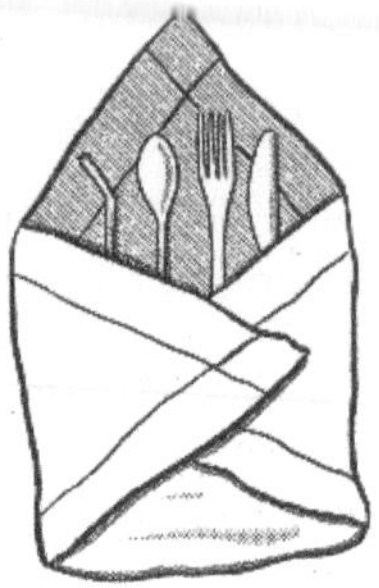

If we were to dig into an urban garbage dump from the last decade, chances are, we will find innumerable plastic spoons, bowls and cups. Why add to this mess? When you're out at a food court, or buying from a street vendor, ask if they serve food in washable plates or other eco-friendly options like banana leaves or stitched leaves. A lot of places serve cutlery made from wood or bagasse, but those are still single-use and create waste that can be avoided. Not to mention, the huge waste of resources that goes into making them. In case of a pandemic situation, unless surface transmission is conclusively proven, using reusable cutlery should be fine.

Of course, there are times when you might really crave to eat at that place that, say, serves delicious pav bhaji but uses disposable plates only. Try carrying your own plate and spoons along with a bottle of water. Sure, some people might stare, but you might end up inspiring a few too!

4.

Bottle it up!

So, you're out at the movies or shopping for a bunch of things. Given the traffic and crowds, you're hungry, thirsty and tired by the time you're done. Carrying a small snack and a bottle of water (that you can refill) is a great way to keep the 'hanger' away. Also, with a pandemic plaguing us, carrying your own bottle is only the more sensible thing to do. This is also helpful during flights and long train or bus journeys. If not, we end up buying the ubiquitous packaged snack and drink, creating plastic waste in the process.

5.

Bottle, bottle everywhere...

A lot of restaurants these days exclusively serve bottled water and say they don't have regular water. Some restaurants that serve only thali meals also offer only bottled water, and brush you aside with a 'But it's free' when you ask for regular water. Explain your concern politely and ask for water that the staff themselves drink. More often than not, they are quite happy to oblige. If not, this is where that bottle of water you carry comes in handy!

6.

Don't forget that shopping list

When we go grocery shopping without a shopping list, we tend to buy things that we do not really need, often tempted by deals and offers (and hunger!). Later, these purchases tend to lie unused and go to waste – and/or just add to packaging waste. Having a clear shopping list also saves time and money, both, as we buy only what we really need. It's a win-win!

7.

Skip the supermarkets for your veggies

You know the case with most supermarkets – if the vegetables aren't already sold shrink-wrapped, you might be expected to put them in separate plastic or paper bags for weighing. Why not skip the waste and buy fresher produce at your local markets instead? If you really have to shop for your veggies and fruits at a supermarket, skip the produce bag and ask for the weight/price sticker to be stuck directly onto your bag or the produce itself.

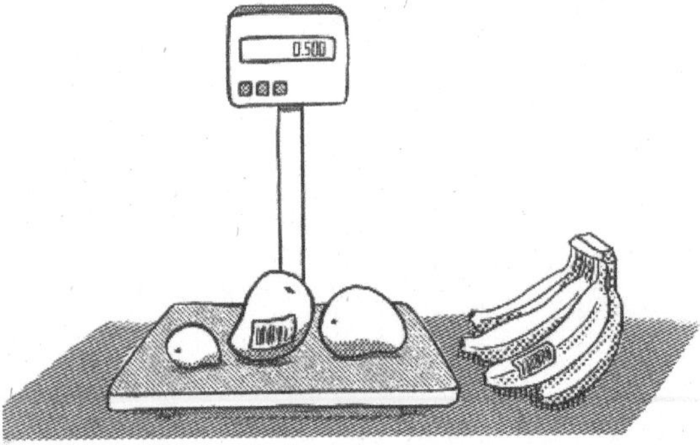

8.

Buy groceries from bulk stores

Try and find stores that sell grocery staples like rice, wheat, dal in bulk, without packaging. You can take your own bags and containers to these stores and buy what you need. It may not be possible to buy everything from bulk stores without plastic packaging all the time, but it's worth doing wherever possible with some pre-planning. It is also a good way to support small local businesses.

9.

Micro greens. Macro joy.

Growing your own food may sound daunting, but it can be quite easy and fun – irrespective of where you live and how much space you have. Be it a huge bungalow or a tiny apartment, you can experiment by growing microgreens as they don't require more than a couple of square feet.

In fact, this is a great activity to do with young children. It doesn't need any special equipment or planters. Reuse coconut shells, takeaway containers, or those thin plastic containers that mushrooms and strawberries are sold in. Line them with a thin layer of soil, or some cotton, sprinkle a small spoonful of the seed you want, and lightly spray water. In a week or so, you'll have a tray full of microgreens. They have high nutritional value – and Instagram value as well!

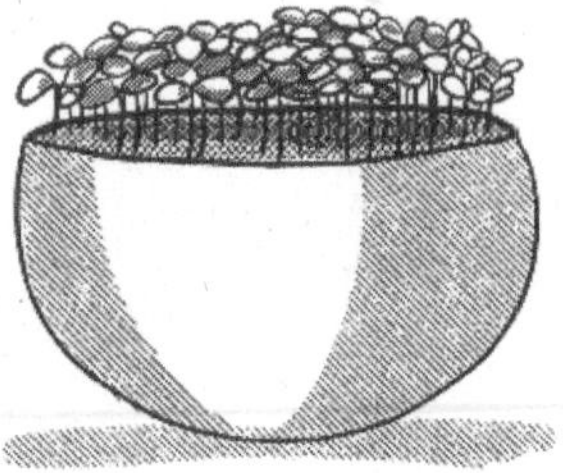

10.

DIY sauces and ketchup

Most condiments, sauces and salad dressings are often sold in plastic sachets or bottles. After usage, most of these sachets and bottles are not recycled as they end up in a landfill as mixed waste. They have preservatives and high sugar or salt content as well. It is much cheaper and healthier to make these items at home in bulk and freeze them. We save money and also avoid creating packaging waste. The internet is full of DIY recipes for everything – from mayonnaise to kasundi – so make the most of it. If the time or inclination to make these yourself is scarce, try and find a friend or someone near you who already does.

11.

Meal Planning = Less Waste

Planning ahead helps reduce waste – not just food waste but ANY waste. Every weekend, try and spend some time to plan your various meals for the week. You can either shop for groceries based on the meal plan you make or vice versa. You could also prep ahead for some dishes and freeze them for use later – example: cooked dal, grated coconut, cooked legumes, etc. If you have pets, meal planning for them helps save time. You can make the main food for your pets and freeze it for use later.

Weekly Meal Plan

	Breakfast	Lunch	Dinner
Mon		Veg. Pulao	Salad
Tue	?	Rice + sambar + carrot stir-fry	Chapati + sambar
Wed	Ragi dose	Order in?	Mushroom stir-fry + pasta
Thurs	Porridge 	Noodles + tofu gravy 	Same as lunch
Fri	Sabudana khichdi	Aloo paratha + chana	Salad
Sat	Poha	Leftovers	
Sun	Banana Pancakes	Pita + hummus + salad	?

12.

Think Local. hyperlocal

You've probably read all about food miles, and why buying food that is grown closer to you is more beneficial to your health and the planet's health too. Now, let's take that one step further. Instead of, say, buying that loaf of bread from a supermarket, find a local bakery. Or look for someone who bakes and sells some in your neighbourhood or apartment complex, if you live in one. And now, with the increase in home businesses during the pandemic, there are a lot of home-based chefs that serve fresh meals on-demand. So, you can look for options around your area if you aren't in the mood to cook. The bonus is that you could possibly carry your own containers too!

13.

Tea ~~bags~~ and coffee ~~sachets~~

Did you know that some tea bags contain plastic coating and do not decompose? They also release microplastics when immersed in hot water. Choosing loose-leaf tea and using a strainer reduces the amount of non-biodegradable waste generated by the bags and sachets, along with the toxic microplastics you might ingest. The case is the same with the instant coffee sachets and single-brew coffee pouches. Opt to buy ground coffee powder that might last much longer instead of ready-to-use capsules or single-serve pouches. The used-up loose tea and coffee grounds are great for your in-home composting project as well.

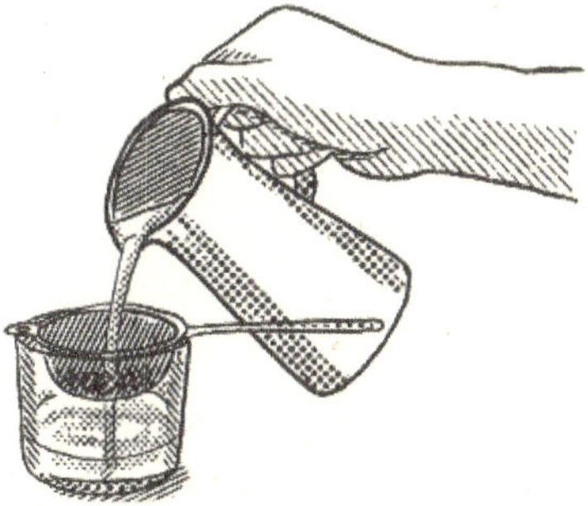

14.

Sustainability takes the cake

Most bakeries add a single-use plastic knife, and candles, when you order a cake for a birthday or an event. The next time you order a cake, you could ask the store to skip packing the plastic knife and instead plan to have a usual steel knife to cut the cake. As more customers insist on no plastic options, they may look for alternatives or simply skip the knife.

15.

Plant-based food FTW!

Plant-based foods emit fewer greenhouse gases than meat and dairy, regardless of how they are produced. On the other hand, cattle, livestock and poultry need to be fed. Then more resources are consumed in the processing, packaging and distribution process as well. Eating plant-based food is much better for the environment than meat and dairy-based food, even if these are sourced locally and transport emissions are not involved. There is no 'one easy template' or solution for reducing your carbon footprint with food. Read up, ask people and learn more about your food and its farm-to-plate journey to make these important decisions. Even if you can start by avoiding meat one day a week, or a few days a week, you'll still be making a significant impact on the planet.

16.

Know your fish. Know your meat.

Talking to your meat and fish vendor and reading up India-specific online resources, such as Know Your Fish, can be very helpful in understanding responsible seafood consumption. It is a voluntary initiative towards an ocean-friendly lifestyle. You can also find a seafood calendar to help you make seasonal and sustainable choices. Even though an average Indian eats much less meat per annum as compared to people in western countries, small changes will make a difference. Where possible, buying from small, local farms is better than factory processed meat and dairy.

17.

MYOJ - Make your own Juice!

Why choose preservative-laden, sugary, plastic-packaged juice that is neither good for us nor for the environment? These multi-layered cartons are very difficult to recycle and languish in our soil and water bodies for several hundred years. Making your own fresh juice at home is healthier too! Even better, consume the fruit as is. It's great for our body and the environment.

18.

Bottle that milk

If you consume milk regularly, and you're buying them in cartons or plastic pouches, consider switching to bottled milk. As more people are seeking eco-friendly options, many small dairy farms are offering milk in bottles which can be returned and reused. Ask around, or look online, and you might find options. If you're still unable to find any, try and save your packets and take them to a recycling agent or your neighbourhood raddiwallah.

19.

Say (Local) cheeeeese!

If cheese is something you like to indulge in, try and source locally-made cheese. Cheese that is made thousands of kilometres away needs preservatives, plastic packaging and also cold storage to reach your nearest supermarket. Ask your friends or trawl through social media to find out local cheesemakers in your city and give them a chance as opposed to the imported stuff.

20.

Multi-layered packaging = multi-layered problem!

- That potato chips packet
- The yummy dark chocolate
- The bhujia that is perfect for munching on a road trip
- That aam panna drink in an easy pack.
- Or that carton of fruit juice!

They all use MLP (Multi-layered packaging) with several different materials that make it difficult to recycle. Most of this packaging waste is never picked up for recycling because they do not bring much value. So, skip food and drink packaged in multi-layered packets wherever possible and instead carry your own, or look for alternatives in eco-friendly packaging or buy in bulk.

21.

Ecobrick in the wall

Of course, there are those instances when plastic invariably creeps into our lives. What do we do with the odd chips packet, polythene bag, chocolate and candy wrappers (MLP waste)? They are refused by many rag pickers/kabadiwalas and only end up in garbage dumps.

You could crush them and stuff them into empty PET bottles and pack them in tight till the bottles become sturdy as a brick. This is called an Ecobrick and can be used to build simple structures in your garden. Eco-bricks are a highly effective, but temporary solution in places where there is neither a plan nor resources to treat single-use plastic, like in remote mountain regions. If you look up Ecobricks on Pinterest, you'll see people have some really creative ideas – from building coffee tables to even houses, they are being used for so many things! This is a constructive way to prevent the plastic waste from ending up in landfills or our water bodies. However, having this option doesn't mean being reckless in our consumption of single-use plastic.

22.

Repurpose old clothing as kitchen rags

Do we really need fancy kitchen paper towel rolls and specially made microfibre and nanofiber cloth? Our parents and grandparents managed to keep their kitchens spic and span without any of those. It is a good idea to go back to those habits. Simply cutting up old worn-out shirts, or even old bedsheets and towels, and using them works just as well. Saves resources and money!

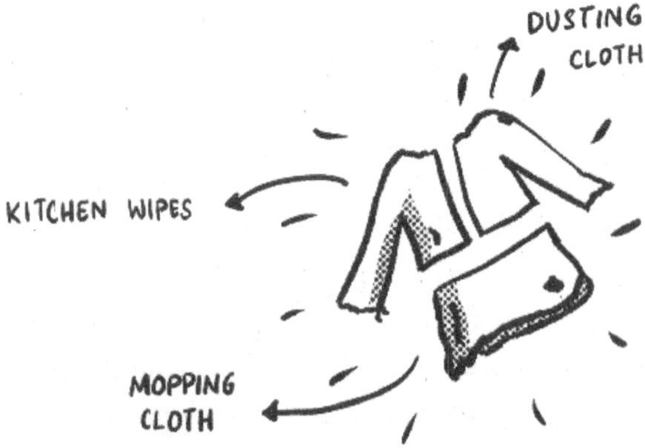

23.

Kombucha is cool, but...

Across various parts of India, there is a traditional method to use up leftover cooked rice that borders on the genius. The leftover cooked rice is soaked overnight in water, thus fermenting it, and the next day, it is seasoned with either salt and lemon, or curd, or served with side dishes depending on the region of origin. It is called *poita bhaat* in Assam, *chaddannam* in Andhra Pradesh and Telangana, *pazhaya soru* in Tamil Nadu or *pakhala bhaat* in Odisha, and the base ingredient for all of them is rice fermented in water. Research has shown that it is rich in probiotics, as well as Vitamin B12, iron, sodium, and potassium. It is also known to be very cooling, perfect for Indian summers. It is quite fascinating to see how some of the ancient wisdom passed onto us from our parents and grandparents is not only healthy, but also zero-waste. So the next time you have a batch of cooked rice leftover from lunch or dinner, don't put it into the fridge – soak it in water and keep it covered, and you have a nutritious breakfast ready for the next day!

②

CLOTHING AND FOOTWEAR

24.

Hit the brakes on fast fashion

Like fast food, fast fashion refers to clothing that is typically cheap and quick to produce. And just like fast food, indulging in fast fashion is not the best choice. Most of these designs are often knock-offs of what is showcased at Fashion Weeks by luxury brands. This also results in several high-street brands releasing new 'collections' as often as every week or every other week, rather than four times a year to match with the seasons. The idea is that the clothing is cheap to make, so it is priced cheaply and people are lured into buying more and buying often. But the 'cheap' clothing is almost always made at a great environmental cost, and the exploitation of human labour.

Shop from brands that have ethical labour practices and make clothing that is meant to last, rather than binge-buying hundreds of cheap clothes a year. Their prices may be high compared to regular brands, but there is often a cost associated with responsible buying. And it may be worth it, if you can afford it. You could also buy fabric from brands such as Khadi and get your clothes stitched by your neighbourhood tailor

BIG BILLION
TWO DAY SHIPPING
BUY ONE GET ONE
FLASH FRIDAY
SAME DAY DELIVERY
FREE RETURNS
70% OFF
50%
FREE SHIPPING
80% OFF
FREE DELIVERY

25.

Take a 'no-buy' pledge

A regular cotton T-shirt requires about 2,700 litres of water to make – that's about three years' worth of drinking water for an adult.

But, often, this statistic and a wardrobe full of clothes slip from our minds when we come across something on sale. Or worse, when that 'nothing to wear' syndrome afflicts us. How about taking a 'no-buy pledge' for the next three months, or six months, or even one whole year, if you're game? This might help you rediscover clothes that you've seldom worn, and save some money too!

Sure, owning a smaller wardrobe and a limited collection of clothing can cramp your style, but get a bit creative and use the vast wisdom of the internet for help. You'll be surprised to discover the many ways in which you can style the same shirt, or even a kurta. Bring out the accessories, the scarves, the belts, and try and mix up things a bit into something new.

26.

Mend It, Beckham!

That button that snapped off, the hem that has come undone, or the seams that have a split? If you don't already know how to make these small repairs, it's a great idea to teach yourself how to. For bigger rips that might need professional help, or a sewing machine, enlist the help of your local tailor. For that rip in your favourite silk shirt, find a professional fabric care or dry cleaning service around you – they are most likely to offer 'darning' services, and will be able to quite neatly patch up small rips in your clothes.

27.

Seek out second-hand/thrift stores

While physical stores selling second-hand clothing are yet to become popular in India, there are a lot of stores popping up online and on social media platforms like Instagram and Facebook. This is a great idea with a twofold benefit – clothes that might languish unworn in a cupboard or end up being thrown out can now find a new owner, who now has a piece of new and unique clothing without too much impact on the planet!

28.

Swap clothing with friends

Have a bunch of friends or family members who have similar taste in clothes and are roughly the same size as you are? How about swapping clothes for a few months to change things up? Even if your tastes are radically different, it might be a fun experiment to sift through each other's wardrobes to see what might catch your eye! You can even use social media to organise such swaps in a group of like-minded people. This is a fun way to spice up your style sustainably.

29.

Park that cart

You've been really good with cutting down on shopping and then one day, out of boredom or curiosity, you go click on one item on your favourite e-commerce website or app. Next thing you know the ads are following you from the browser to your app and into your head. Here's a way to deal with that temptation – add it to your cart and leave it there. For 30 days. If you still want to get it after 30 days, go for it. If not, you didn't need it in the first place. Also, make sure to clear cookies and your browser data from time to time to prevent these temptations from popping up – beat the algorithm! Or simply delete shopping apps from your phone!

Know your fibres!

Synthetic clothing releases millions of tiny microfibres into the air and water with every load of laundry. These microfibres are ingested by marine life and eventually end higher up the food chain and in our bodies too. Moreover, they tend to absorb toxic matter from water and are one of the biggest sources of ocean pollution. So, are natural fibres the way to go? Not exactly, because fabrics like cotton are water and pesticide-intensive and some fabrics heavily use toxic chemicals for their processing. (A pair of jeans can use up to 10,000 litres of water, we've learnt.) Then, short of going au naturel, what are our options? Recycled natural fibres, buying less and taking very good care of our clothing seems to be the most ideal option so far.

30.

Washing and drying clothes

If you often use a washing machine, ensure that you understand the settings so that less energy and water is wasted. Also, where possible, try to use a natural, plant-based, biodegradable laundry powder or soapnut-based liquid. Avoid using detergent powders, liquid and fabric softeners that contain microbeads (which are nothing but tiny plastic beads). Wherever you can, air/sun dry your clothes instead of using the machine dryer to prolong the life of your clothes. Darker clothes have the advantage of needing fewer washes because, unlike light-coloured clothing, slight soiling doesn't show up.

31.

Wash with care

Yes, we know that synthetic fabrics release a lot of microfibres but, let's face it, nothing beats the convenience of these fabrics for workout wear and swimwear. In these cases, taking great care while washing goes a long way in curtailing the microfibers released as well as in increasing the life of your garments.

- Hand-wash garments when possible so that fewer microfibres are released.
- Wash synthetic garments together so the friction is reduced.
- If you are using a washing machine, try and wash the same kind of fabrics together, again, to reduce friction.

32.

Switch out the plastic clips/ clothes pegs

Sun-drying our clothes is fantastic and nothing beats the fragrance of laundry that has soaked up some sunshine and fresh air. The same cannot be said of the plastic clips that we use to fasten the clothes to the line. After several months of usage, they tend to become brittle and crumble to pieces. A more durable and eco-friendly option is to look for wooden or metal alternatives.

33.

These old boots

Most commercially available footwear is difficult to recycle. Millions of shoes end up in dump yards, landfills and water bodies every year in India. This happens despite our culture of repairing and reusing footwear. It is a good idea to buy a good-quality pair that will last long. And instead of discarding footwear at the slightest problem, prolonging its life by mending it helps prevent more footwear from ending up in the garbage.

Greenwashing Alert!

Greenwashing refers to the practice of intentionally misleading customers into believing that a product or a company is environmentally responsible. You might have seen some campaigns by big fast fashion brands that reward you with vouchers in lieu of clothes donated to charity. In many cases, the clothes end up in landfills while the brand has found yet another way to lure the customer to come back to their store with the vouchers. This is greenwashing. You might also have seen FMCG goods being advertised as 'Herbal', 'Eco-friendly' and '100% Natural' without any solid backing to these claims. Or clothing brands that use popular jargon like 'ethical and sustainable' without really telling you more. These are all forms of greenwashing. Beware!

3

PERSONAL CARE

34.

Kick the bottle!

The shampoo bottle, that bottle of body wash, that bottle of conditioner – somewhere along the way it became cooler to use these personal care products that come in liquid form in plastic bottles, instead of the products we used in the past. Consider switching back to that old-fashioned soap (the hand-made range available now is quite mind-blowing), to reetha over shampoo, or even a shampoo bar. Though it may be difficult to kick this habit off at once, you could take a pledge to remove at least ONE item from your bathroom that comes in plastic packaging. These are some basic switches we can make without stepping too far out of our comfort zones.

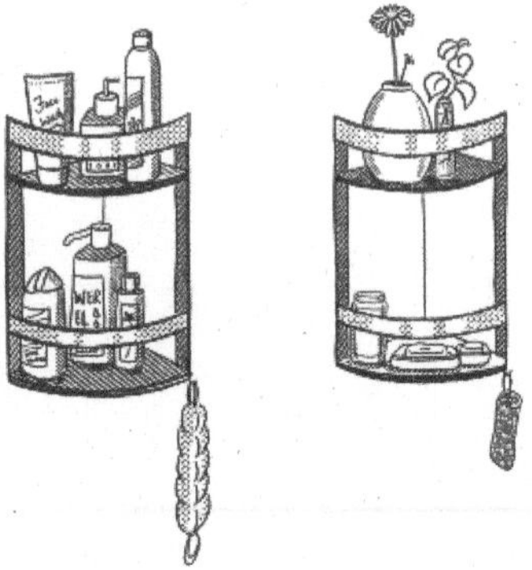

35.

Multipurpose make-up

What if instead of buying a dozen different make-up products, we could have a few items and use them in several ways? For example, that lip balm can double up as blush on your cheeks, while your compact/pressed face powder can double up as a foundation and even turn your glossy lipstick matte. Invest in products that can be used in multiple ways. Not only is it better for the environment, but you also save money, and this way, the chances of your make-up being fully used up before expiring are high!

36.

Banish body odour the green way

As sustainable and earth-friendly as we'd want to be, most of us might draw the line at giving up deodorants, plastic packaging notwithstanding. Alum/fitkari, the naturally available salt (chemical compound potassium aluminium sulphate), is a very effective deodorant with antimicrobial properties. Alternatively, a mixture of coconut oil, baking soda, arrowroot powder can also be used as a replacement for deodorant. Natural deodorants are also better than chemical-based aerosol sprays that may cause respiratory issues.

37.

The trooothpaste

It's quite mindboggling to imagine the number of toothpaste tubes that we've possibly used and thrown until now. Because toothpaste tubes are not recyclable, they end up in landfills. Once upon a time, before toothpaste and tubes came into being, people would use tooth powder that came in tin containers, but there are plenty of other options now if you're looking to be eco-friendly. To start with, you can make your own – some recipes available on the internet barely take a few minutes! If you haven't already made the switch to a wooden/ bamboo toothbrush, it's probably a good idea to buy a few of those in bulk as well. Bamboo has a much lower footprint than plastics, is very quick to grow (it is a grass!) and can be reused as wood.

38.

Wash, Rinse, Segregate

Most personal care and beauty products are packaged in plastic containers. What do we do when the product is over? Do NOT throw them away as it is. Rinse in warm water and dry them before segregating and handing them over to your local kabadiwala or a Material Recovery Facility. This simple act ensures better recyclability and returns for those employed in the entire waste processing chain.

39.

Make some noise about earbuds

A lot of noise is made about single-use plastic straws, but an often-forgotten piece of plastic that is used once and tossed away is the humble earbud. There are alternatives to plastic – bamboo and paper, most commonly. Whatever you use, make sure you don't flush them down the toilet, though. They end up making their way through sewage and into our seas. Remember that iconic photo of the sea horse around an earbud?

40.

Smooth shave

Traditionally, stainless steel razors and knives were used for shaving. They were sterilized in hot water and disinfectant, and reused. But with the proliferation of brands offering disposable razors – with triple and more blades, promoted by attractive advertising campaigns – millions switched to these disposable options, which contributes to non-biodegradable waste more than you can imagine, It is a good time to switch back to reusable steel razors. We can prevent hundreds of thousands of plastic disposable razors from ending up in landfills.

41.

The butt problem

Every day, crores and crores of cigarette butts are carelessly tossed all around by smokers. Many end up starting fires and/or clogging waterways and staying in our soil, not decomposing for hundreds of years. We do not even need to talk about the enormous impact of tobacco (active as well as passive smoking), and the plastic packaging involved, on our health and the planet. So, how does one solve this problem? The only solution is to quit smoking. There is no such thing as responsible smoking.

42.

Ditch the disposable pads

Disposable sanitary pads and tampons are not biodegradable. And often filled with nasty chemicals that aren't great for our bodies or our planet. Reusable cloth sanitary napkins are a good alternative. Menstrual cups are another fantastic option to consider. These options are also far more economical in the long run as compared to disposable sanitary pads and tampons.

A menstrual cup can last upto 10 years.

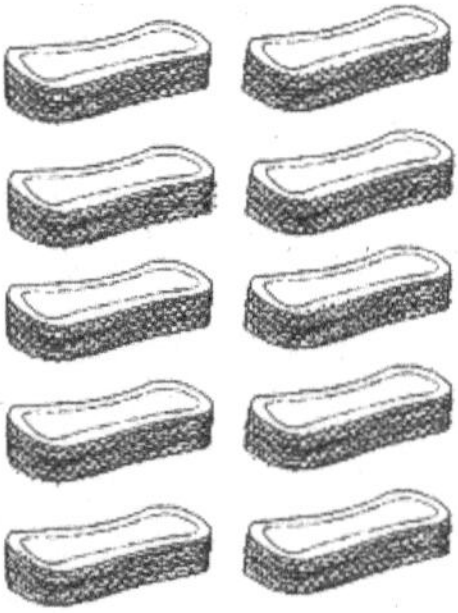

One person can use upto 1,200 pads over 10 years.

43.

Skip those wet wipes!

Most wet wipes in the Indian market are made with non-woven polypropylene and are not biodegradable. And obviously, they are not compostable either. They could potentially end up clogging sewers or in our waterways. It is a good idea to skip them and choose reusable alternatives such as cloth pads or muslin wipes. Do a web search on 'Fatberg London' to see the damage wet wipes can cause when flushed down toilets.

44.

Sheet masks? Nope!

Sheet masks have been all the rage in the past few years for the wonders they can do to our skin. The bad news is that they are not biodegradable and, hence, not good for our planet. The pouches they come in are invariably made of multi-layered packaging. What are some alternatives? Home-made face masks with any of these ingredients like fruit, egg, cream, multani mitti or fuller's earth, rosewater, etc., are just some of the options, and traditional recipes always work like a charm!

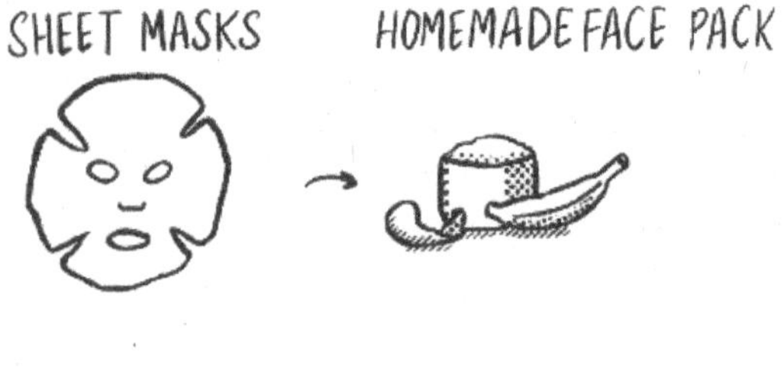

④

IN AND AROUND THE HOUSE

45.

Segregate the waste you generate

Understanding and segregating waste at the source (of generation) is the most basic way to get started. In simple terms, we have to separate the waste into:

- Compostable/Organic Waste (kitchen and garden waste). This can be used to make your own compost at home.
- Dry Waste (plastic, paper, metal, glass and e-waste). These need to be in separate bags or boxes for easy recycling.
- Reject Waste (sanitary waste, sharp objects, construction debris, etc.). These need to be handled as per your local government's instructions.

If we do not segregate this waste at the home/apartment/street/community level, they get dumped into garbage mounds and landfills, and remain there for several centuries.

46.

Do a waste audit

'What you do not measure, you cannot manage' is a pretty popular quote in business and management circles. How about adapting it to waste management? How about measuring the amount of waste you generate in the period of one month?

Have separate bins for plastic, glass, metal, e-waste, wood, Styrofoam/thermocol and organic waste at home. You will begin to see the most common type of waste you generate, and then you can figure out how to manage it. Label the bins at home and get everyone to help by throwing the waste in the appropriate bins.

47.

Vinegar + Baking Soda = Magic!

It's amazing to see just how versatile these everyday kitchen ingredients can be. Sure, we all did those volcano experiments in school, but have you tried out this fantastic combination to clean the grease from a sticky chimney hob, a stove or some dishes? To clear a drain or clean a bathroom? Instead of spending a small fortune on a multitude of cleaning products, try these two and then stock up in bulk.

48.

Bio enzymes

Take things one step further and make your own vinegar for cleaning, from vegetable and fruits scraps. This is commonly called a bio enzyme. This is an incredibly fascinating process where you combine peels, sugar and water and let the entire mixture sit in an airtight container in the dark for about a couple of months. At the end of this period, thanks to natural microbial action, the water has morphed into a powerful cleaning agent that is completely non-toxic.

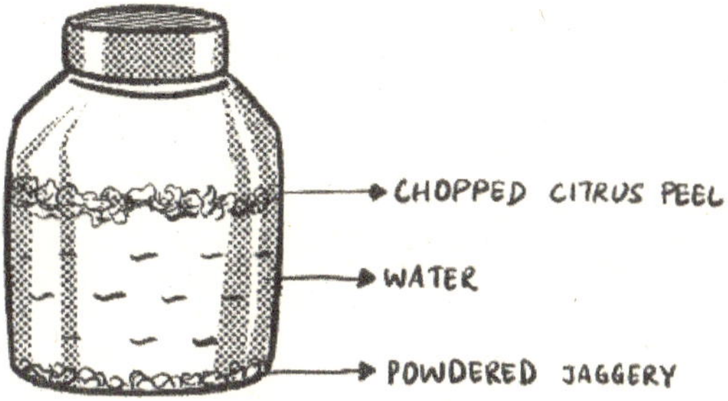

49.

Let the plastic brush go

The good thing about the world sitting up and taking notice of the zero-waste movement, and it becoming trendy (thanks to social media!), is that a lot of alternatives to the standard mass-manufactured goods are now easily available. So, where plastic brushes were the only option for cleaning sinks, tiles and bathrooms, there are now several brands making wooden brushes and even coconut coir scrubbers for dishes!

50.

Ditch that cling film

Cling film is a fascinating invention, no doubt, but do we really need to store food in a bowl and cover it with a couple of layers of cling film? It is not recyclable. How about simply putting a well-fitting lid on it instead? Rather than wrapping half-used vegetables or fruit in clingfilm, storing them in an airtight container will be just as effective, without the wastage. Or you could get beeswax wraps too, but they also have a limited life before the wax coating wears off.

51.

Diapers for children

When it comes to diapering, there are plenty of eco-friendly alternatives to a non-biodegradable disposable diaper. At one end of the range, we have the humble home-made cloth diaper, and at the other, we have the water-proof modern cloth diaper that can be used from infancy and adjusted to fit until toddlerhood. These also come in quite an expansive range of colours and prints. While it is a sizeable investment initially, it is definitely more economical than using 6-8 disposable diapers per day, and are infinitely better for the environment.

52.

Pray, rethink that room spray

Even today, crores of Indians use traditional frankincense, natural agarbatti and other natural substances to add fragrance to their house or places of worship. But there has been a glut of cheaply available, well-marketed aerosol canisters/sprays with chemical 'room fresheners' or car perfume. Not only do they generate a mountain of waste but are also harmful for the lungs due to the chemicals in them. Skip these aerosols and choose natural products such as incense, potpourri, sandal powder or even charcoal (to absorb odour) instead. Save your lungs and the environment!

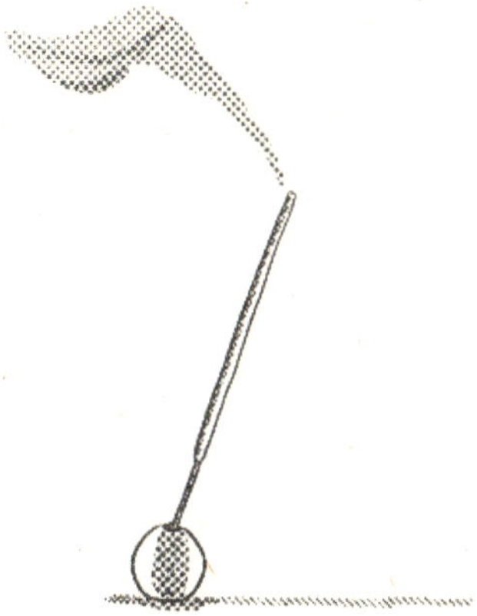

53.

Fix a mist nozzle in your water taps

Be it brushing our teeth, shaving, washing our face or vegetables, we often use much more water than what we need. Over the course of an entire year it adds up to thousands of litres of water wasted down the drain. Fixing an aerator/mist nozzle on the water taps greatly reduces the amount of water used by aerating the water into a fine mist which gets the job done. It is a small investment to make initially but it saves a ton of water and money in the long run.

54.

Garbage bags are garbage

It is a tragedy that to carry garbage, we create more garbage by using a bin liner or a plastic/ polythene garbage bag. Every day millions of these bags get thrown away, creating more and more plastic pollution. If we learn to segregate and collect our waste at the source, there is no need to use garbage bin liners or bags.

And no. Do not fall for 'greenwashing' terms such as bio-liners, bio bags, biodegradable bin bags, eco-friendly bin liners, etc. These are still largely plastic bags, which most likely will not be compostable in a home compost bin or a landfill and may take several decades to break down. And only into tinier and tinier pieces of microplastic. That's all.

55.

Don't throw e-waste in the trash bin

Indians generate lakhs of tonnes of electronic waste every year and most of it ends up in municipal bins meant for domestic biodegradable waste. Why be a part of this problem when you can easily segregate this waste at the source? Keep a separate bin at home (or office) to collect electronic/electrical waste such as batteries, junk computer parts, bulbs, charger cables, etc. Hand it over to organisations like SONY/Croma e-waste collection initiatives, Namo eWaste, etc., that handle e-waste as per norms.

56.

Buy rechargeable gadgets

When shopping for gadgets, look for those with the option of a built-in rechargeable battery. Then throughout their lifetime, we will have saved hundreds of batteries from ending up in a landfill. If they do not have a built-in battery – for instance in devices like cameras, flash lights, etc. – try to use rechargeable AA/AAA type batteries to curb the waste.

57.

Composting is magical

After segregating your wet and dry waste, put the organic wet waste into a pit in your garden, or use an old bucket or a composting bin/pot (example: Khamba from DailyDump.org), and add dry leaves or coco peat for absorbing moisture. There is a ton of content online on composting (example: DailyDump, Vani Murthy's social media channels) to help you get started. The compost you get as a result is just gold! It is rich in nutrients and helps your plants grow well. The satisfaction of having no organic waste leave your house is something else!

58.

Reuse your greywater

If you have an RO system at home, you can prevent a substantial amount of water from being wasted by reusing the discarded water. You could use it to water plants, or to mop the floor, or to clean bathrooms and sinks. You can also keep a bucket next to your kitchen sink to collect water that you discard from washing your hands, and even vegetables and greens. This water can again be used for cleaning the sink or watering your plants.

59.

Befriend your local raddiwallah

Yes, those cartons from some online shopping, or those plastic packets that you probably got some pre-packed groceries in, those glass bottles, curd or yoghurt tubs and whatever other packaging waste you might collect through the month – save them in a big container or a plastic bag, and at the end of every month take them to your local raddiwallah to exchange them for some cash. Or look up companies that offer dry waste pick-up from your doorstep – there are plenty of those cropping up now. The chances of things getting recycled are much, much higher when you hand them over to a recycling service or a raddiwallah, rather than just throwing them into the garbage bin.

60.

Stop cutting corners. *Literally.*

Milk sachets. Oil sachets. These days everything is packaged in sachets and pouches. When opening them, we often end up snipping the edge completely to make a hole in the sachet/pouch and throw away that piece along with the rest of the packet. What happens to those millions of small triangular snipped pieces that are thrown away? They end up in the soil and water and are never collected for recycling. So, do not cut the sachet or pouch fully but only make 3/4th of a cut so that the cut piece hangs on to the full sachet/pouch. This small mindfulness goes a long way.

61.

Pet toys and accessories

Good quality toys and accessories for pets can be expensive. Why not borrow or buy second hand? Find out from your friends and social media network if anyone has toys, leashes, bowls, plates, beds, safety gates, etc., lying around that they can sell or lend to you. Not only will this be cheaper, but also better for the environment.

Choose toys, leashes, collars and beds made from natural material instead of plastics that can be harmful and toxic. When you buy anything new, invest in good quality, sturdy accessories that will last a long time. This means you can either sell them or give them away when your pet no longer needs them.

62.

Pet food and treats

The best pet food is something that you can cook yourself based on the recommendations of the veterinarian. If you do not have the time or energy to cook daily, you could do meal planning: cook and freeze for a week. Or you could consider signing up for a pet food subscription service.

If you have to buy pet food, consider buying it in bulk so you only have one big sack or packet of plastic when the food is over. This big sack or bag (usually sturdy) can be reused multiple times to store things or can be upcycled into bags and pouches.

63.

Check the Energy Star Ratings

Check the Energy Star rating of your appliances provided by the Bureau of Energy Efficiency (BEE) and learn more about the energy consumption of various products. When you are looking to buy a new appliance, always pay attention to this rating (it is a prominently placed sticker on the appliance) and do not get tempted by offers, freebies and discounts by salespeople. Investing some extra money in an energy-saving appliance will be beneficial in the long run with lower electricity bills.

64.

Bring back the fountain pen

Given that ball-point pens and their refills are made of plastic, investing in a nice fountain pen instead of buying disposable pens each time we run out of ink is a good idea. If you don't want to be bothered about filling up ink, you could invest in one good quality ball-point pen that you can buy refills for. Similarly, refilling is the way to go for whiteboard markers as well. Instead of buying disposable markers, opt for refillable ones. The idea is the same – how can we get as close to zero-waste as possible?

Pro tip – store your markers upside down to let the ink flow to the nib side, prolonging the life of the marker.

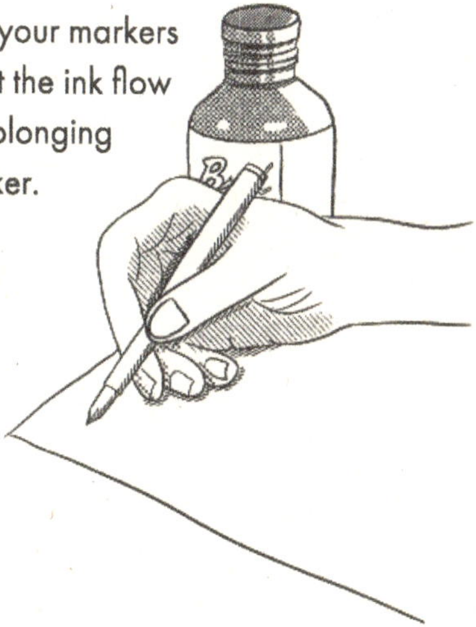

5

OUTSIDE THE HOUSE

65.

Run your errands

Stepping out for an errand that's less than a couple of kilometres from the house? Why not walk or cycle to your destination instead of taking the car or your two-wheeler? Sure, it might seem time-consuming, but if we plan our errands, route and time wisely, it gets easier. This is also a super-efficient way of adding some light cardio to your day. The planet and your body will be grateful.

66.

Commuting to work

Commutes to work in our cities are invariably slow in the thick of traffic. The thing is, we seldom realise that we are the traffic that we complain about. Cycling is an eco-friendly way to commute, and there are several electric cycle options available these days as well. But if that is not feasible for you because of your commuting distance or other factors, how about being part of a carpool? It helps reduce the number of vehicles out on the roads, as well as the pollution levels and your carbon footprint. The good thing is that there are quite a few app-based pool or ride-sharing options, so it should be fairly easy to find one around you. What's more – you can also make some buddies outside of your workplace! While this may not be feasible when a pandemic is raging, and there are strict social distancing rules, this is definitely an option worth considering in a non-pandemic situation.

67.

That meeting could've been an email

With the Covid-19 pandemic, a lot of businesses have woken up to the fact that those 'urgent' and 'unavoidable' business trips can be avoided, to a large extent. The distinction between essential and non-essential has become clear now. Hopefully, even in the post-Covid world, there will be lesser non-essential travel, and working from home will become mainstream. If, in the future, you have the power to make a decision about work-related travel, it maybe a good idea to assess if it can be done virtually, and keep the carbon footprint low.

68.

Event freebies

At pretty much every event or conference that you attend, there will invariably be freebies. It can be anything – a pen, a water bottle, a notebook, t-shirt, pen-drive, a bag, etc. Do you really need any of those? Are feelings going to get hurt if you politely say no, thank them and smile? You will save a bunch of clutter from being brought into the house by doing so. Eventually, the hope is that a lot of us will say no, and these freebies will become a thing of the past.

69.

Your mental checklist: the sustainable edition

While heading out of the house, we usually check if we have our phone, wallet and keys, but it's also worth taking an extra minute to also carry a spare grocery bag, a refillable bottle of water, a handkerchief and a snack to prevent the need to buy stuff available in single-use plastics. Add these to your mental checklist and it'll soon become a habit, and you'll be surprised at how much of a difference this makes in the long run!

- [x] Phone, Wallet, Keys
- [x] Water Bottle
- [x] Grocery Bag
- [x] Handkerchief
- [x] Snack

70.

No plastic straws, please!

Though we are beginning to see a big shift in this regard, where more and more businesses are either providing paper straws or skipping them entirely, lakhs of small vendors in India still provide plastic straws. While placing the order for a drink, stress this twice, 'We do not want a plastic straw'. If you cannot make do without a straw, carrying your own reusable straw is a good idea, both in terms of hygiene and the environment. Also, paper straws aren't the best replacement for plastic straws – can you imagine the amount of resources that go into making these paper straws which will probably be used for 10–15 minutes at the most? Do you think that is justified?

71.

Chai or Juice break? Say no to the paper/plastic cup

Chai breaks are everyone's favourite part of the work day. We go to the roadside tapri/chai place and have chai or coffee in a paper cup. If it's paper, it is biodegradable, right? Wrong. These so-called paper cups come lined with a plastic liner or wax coating to make them water-proof. Plastic and Styrofoam cups are even worse. Pouring a hot beverage into these will cause the plastic to leach into it. Avoid these cups, and either ask for a glass tumbler if available or simply carry your own.

72.

The problem with takeaway food

Takeaway food is invariably delivered in plastic or polythene or foil pouches. This is understandable. It is difficult to pack typical liquid/semi liquid Indian food in eco-friendly disposable containers. Technology hasn't progressed enough yet to make viable packaging options that can hold hot/warm food and be eco-friendly at the same time. An easy alternative to this is to bring your own containers to pick up food. If there are restaurants that still use the old-school combination of banana leaves and newspaper, or areca nut or bagasse alternatives, that could be an option. For sweets and bakery items, you can choose butter paper or brown paper bags over plastic if the option is available. The best option, though, would be to carry your own containers.

73.

The humble handkerchief

Over the last few decades, it became uncool to carry a handkerchief and, somehow, it made sense to casually use and dispose of tissues that take tons of resources to make. We've all been guilty of this behaviour. Handkerchiefs are inexpensive and, if you carry one or two with you all the time, you could avoid using those paper tissues offered everywhere. It is not only hygienic but also saves thousands of tissues over the years from going to waste.

BLOOD. SWEAT. TEARS.

THE HANKY'S GOT YOU COVERED.

74.

Zero-waste festivals

It is not easy, but it is definitely possible to gradually go zero-waste while celebrating festivals in India.

Firecrackers are not good for our respiratory systems, not good for our planet, and least of all for those who make them. These can be done away with. If making sweets and savouries at home is an option, pick that over store-bought goodies. If not, look for home-based businesses that make these and patronise them. Instead of using single-use plastic or aluminium containers, you can distribute sweets and savouries in a simple steel plate or bowl, covered with a clean kitchen towel or a new, large handkerchief instead of cling wrap. Choose flowers for decoration if you must, but replace the paper and plastic buntings with beautiful reusable cloth buntings/toran. There are lots of entrepreneurs making these from scrap fabric these days.

75.

Trash and burn?

Burning waste (incineration) has gained popularity around the world with the coming of Waste-to-Energy plants. However, the emissions filled with dioxins and residual ash are quite hazardous to the air and soil. While the jury is out on how these emissions are managed, closer home, we often see small heaps of trash being burnt by the roadside. The smoke from the burning of waste is toxic and can cause several respiratory issues. Make sure you're segregating your waste and disposing it of responsibly so that it is not treated in this manner.

76.

Stacks of bills? No, thank you!

When you make purchases at shops that offer this option, choose to get your bill/invoice via email instead of printing it. A majority of shoppers choosing an emailed digital bill instead of a printed bill every year can save so much ink and paper. And digital bills are easy to save, find and keep track of. The same goes for credit card slips. Many POS machines also offer the option of messaging or emailing the Credit/Debit card slip. So, opt for those when you are out and about.

77.

Coir > Plastic

Coir is a wonderful thing. Ok zoom out! The coconut tree is a miracle! Literally every part of it is useful to us in our low-waste journey. Coir pots or jute bags can be used to grow plants instead of plastic pots or 'grow bags'. The coir and coco peat retain moisture naturally and are bio-degradable whereas plastic bags and pots break down into microplastics over the years and get into our waterbodies. So if you have a balcony garden or a house with a garden, this is definitely a swap that can be easily made.

6

TRAVEL AND FITNESS

78.

Reusable tiffin box with reusable cutlery

This ubiquitous combination can avoid a lot of waste from being generated, especially when we travel. Keeping a set of these along with a handkerchief or two in a bag can serve many purposes, like getting takeaway food, or packing leftovers after a restaurant meal, or simply having the reusable option ready when presented with disposable alternatives.

79.

Always plan your travel essentials

If we do not plan ahead when we travel, we often end up buying cheap, single-use things – toiletries, clothes, accessories, food, etc. Not only do we end up creating a lot more carbon footprint than usual, we also might find ourselves spending more as well. It's usually the small things – toothbrush, phone charger, earphones, socks – that we might miss. So, having a standard packing list really helps.

80.

Vacation closer to home

Let's admit it: flights are the major reason behind carbon emissions in the modern world and every time we take a flight, we are responsible for the environmental damage it causes. So, in the long run, it would be better for the planet (and our wallets) to find and choose places that are closer to our home and can be accessed by public transport or our own pooled vehicles instead of flights. If your wanderlust conflicts with your sustainability, make a compromise – replace at least every other trip to a distant land with someplace that's closer.

81.

Skip airline or train food

Think about airline meals. Most of the food is packaged in cling wrap and/or plastic containers. And many airlines have switched to single-use cutlery as well to keep it easy for the flight crew and others who package the meals. For long haul flights, every snack or meal comes packaged in single-use plastics. So, for every flight we take we generate a lot of waste on top of all the carbon emissions. The same goes for many trains in India. One simple solution to avoid generating all that waste is to eat well before boarding the flight/train and/or carry a meal or some snacks or dry fruits in washable containers or biodegradable packaging (that are accepted by the airport security).

82.

Skip the single-use hotel toiletries

Carrying your own toiletries in mini, refillable bottles (you could use some old containers for this) during travel saves so many plastic bottles from ending up in a landfill. It is surely tempting to pick up and carry back the mini toiletries provided for 'free' at hotels, but think about it – all that only encourages and adds to the plastic waste in your community, since these items are not greatly sought after at recycling facilities. If you have any lying around, do not throw them out. Wash, rinse clean, refill and reuse them when you travel next.

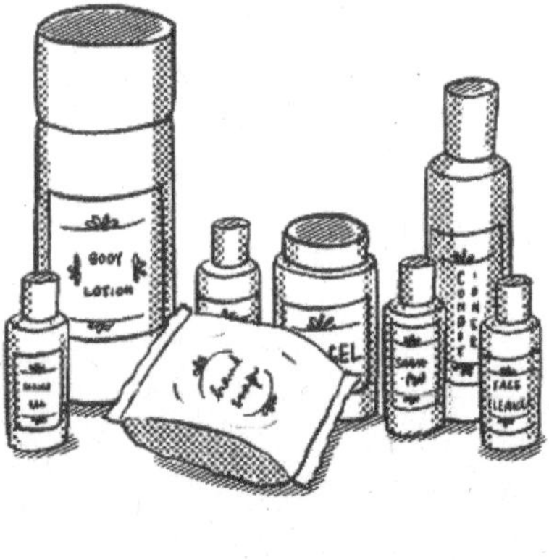

83.

Carry a mini water kettle

Nobody wants to fall sick, least of all when we travel. So it's understandable that a lot of us want to rely on bottled water to be on the safe side. But the amount of plastic waste this generates on a week-long trip can be quite a bit! One alternative to this is to buy 5 or 10 litre bottles or cans and refill smaller bottles. But a much better alternative is to carry a travel-friendly, mini water kettle. It may seem like a minor inconvenience but the benefits are plenty. It also helps to call the hotel ahead of your trip and ensure they will provide a water kettle in the room and filtered water in a jug to the guests. If not, carry your own.

84.

Pledge not to leave behind trash

Most places that attract tourists are vulnerable to destruction due to the land, water and air pollution caused by visitors. (Not to mention tree trunks and rocks being defaced by lovestruck individuals!) When you plan your travel, take a pledge to generate very little waste and also try to carry back the waste you directly generate (food wrappers, packaging, etc.), especially if you're going on a trek to a remote location or an eco-sensitive place such as the hills or the islands.

The idea is to limit our impact on a place we are visiting and preserving its glory.

85.

Consume Less Resources

Goa. Shimla. Ooty. Munnar. Manali. Leh. The story is the same. These places are struggling with the impact of mindless tourism. Their valuable resources like groundwater, topsoil, etc., are fast depleting and tourism is a major reason for that. When you visit any such place – be it for work or for leisure – take a pledge to be sensitive, mindful and to consume less and save more. Stay for longer durations and support the local economy. Take public transport instead of adding to the traffic there. Do not support animal tourism. No one may see your actions, and they may not be immediately quantifiable, but it is important to do this to not burden these destinations.

86.

Invest in good quality travel gear

Invest in good quality luggage, travel accessories and fitness gear even if they are expensive (as long as you can afford that initial investment!). These last longer, can be repaired or exchanged under warranty and you avoid creating waste by discarding and buying new gear every few years. Even though natural fibre-based fitness apparel are good, apparel made with artificial fibre such as polyester or polyamide are extremely durable and, hence, are a worthwhile investment.

87.

Look for green hotels

Green Hotels are hotels that focus on and implement environment-friendly ideas such as no plastic water bottles as a default, waste segregation, organic waste composting, recycling, linen reuse, reduction in packaged food, usage of solar energy and so on. By choosing such hotels, we reduce our carbon footprint while travelling, and also encourage hotel businesses to adopt eco-friendly practices.

88.

Switch up your car freshener

Car fresheners (like room freshener sprays) are made of chemicals and are neither good for our health nor for the environment. Choose natural potpourri, flowers and other natural fresheners such as frankincense instead of chemicals. If you like the smell of coffee, you can also keep used and dried coffee grounds in your car in an old sock. Coffee absorbs any odours and there will be the light fragrance of coffee in the air. They can be used in your fridge or to deodorize a dustbin as well.

89.

Zero-waste buddies

As rewarding as the zero-waste journey is, it can get lonely and difficult at times. This is where having a community really helps. Whether it is to go for a holiday, reach out for recommendations for local stores, borrow tools or clothes, having a like-minded group, preferably in your neighbourhood, can be a great way to keep going and make it easier on ourselves.

7

EVENTS AND GIFTS

90.

Out is in!

An indoor venue needs air conditioning, lighting and lots of decoration that add to the cost and the carbon footprint. Where possible, choosing an outdoor venue, preferably with a varied seating arrangement in a leafy environment, can make your carbon footprint substantially lower. Even in a pandemic situation, this option works well since there is fresh air and lots of physical distance.

91.

Plan backwards

Planning backwards from the end of the event helps greatly in figuring out all the waste that is avoidable. There are some easy ones, like reusable glasses and plates instead of disposables (even if they are made of leaves), and some not so easy ones, like decorations, food and gifts. Decide what you want to do with leftover food – donating the unused food is an option while another option is to send some back with each of the guests. If all the planning and execution of a zero/low waste-event is hard, you also have the alternative to outsource this aspect to organizations that take care of this end to end.

92.

Borrow or rent instead of buying

From the utensils needed for cooking to cutlery, to the decorations to clothing and jewellery, you can rent or borrow virtually anything these days. This not only saves you money but also reduces wasteful consumption and unnecessary extravagance. There are several groups of people coming together to start cutlery banks to rent out batches of cutlery for small scale parties and home-based events. You can look for such initiatives around you. If you're having a small gathering at home, you could ask your guests to bring some of their crockery and cutlery so you won't need to buy disposables or look for other options.

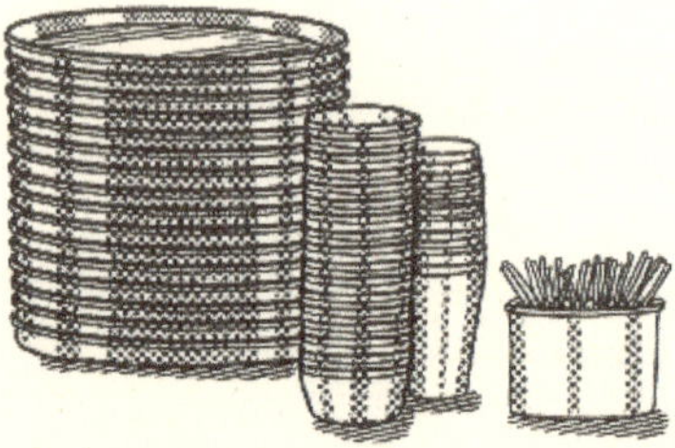

93.

Make it cool – talk about the 'why'

Caring for the environment and not generating waste is kindness. And kindness is cool. Quite often, people may mistake this for 'saving money'. So, it is imperative to explain the 'why' behind our decisions to ditch plastic and other disposables while organizing an event. When the various stakeholders and guests understand the reason, they are more likely to appreciate it. You can put up prominent placards at your venue explaining the low/zero-waste nature of your event. These could be on cute blackboards, written with chalk.

94.

Choose eco-friendly decorations

It may not seem like much, but glittery polythene confetti, balloons, foam boards and similar decorative party props add up to sizeable amounts of non-biodegradable waste every single day. All that waste ends up in our soil and waterways, eventually breaking down into microplastic particles and ending up on our plate inside our food. Avoid synthetic decorations as far as possible, and choose locally available flowers and leaves instead. You could make lovely confetti by punching out dried leaves of various shapes, sizes and colours. There are plenty of fabric streamers available these days, usually made from scrap fabric that are totally worth investing in as well. Not only are they reusable, they also have the added bonus of preventing fabric scraps from ending up in landfills.

95.

Read the signs – naturally!

Fancy props, flexi banners and sign boards are often single-use and end up in the landfill after an event. Use a chalkboard or a green board that can be easily returned after the event. Or use cloth-based signboards. One can also use leaves, flowers and natural paints on cloth to make pretty banners. In South India, kolam powder/rice flour paste is used for decoration. Every region and culture in India has some simple and natural ideas for decorations and signboards. Just ask the seniors in the family, 'What did you do in the '60s and '70s before thermocol and plastic became mainstream?' – and you'll have your answer.

96.

Anticipate. Reduce. Segregate.

Try to anticipate and plan for the amount of waste that will be generated in an event. If possible, outsource this to a professional waste management company or team. Try to appoint someone within the family or company to oversee this exclusively. Having a plan for waste disposal and accordingly having containers marked to hold the segregated waste with clear instructions will help with the process. Weddings and other events generate mammoth amounts of waste – planning can help prevent this to a huge extent.

97.

Wrap gifts in newspaper or cloth

Gift wrapping made from polythene or plastic-laced paper sheets are pretty but live a fleeting single-use life. Most often, after being ripped open, these gift wrap sheets are discarded. Even if they are reused, their life span is short. And then they end up in landfills, remaining there for several hundred years. Choose wisely. Old newspapers, seed papers, scraps of fabric and jute twine are great for gift wrapping. You can even use pressed leaves and flowers to embellish your gifts.

98.

Zero-waste kits as gifts

For those taking their initial steps into zero-waste living, you could put together a few kits to help them along. A personal care kit is a great option. It can have a DIY bathing powder, or handmade soap, shaving alum, shampoo bar or soapnut powder, natural loofah and a bamboo toothbrush. Or it can be a stationery kit! You could get some seed paper pens and pencils and elephant poo paper, and put these together in an upcycled box. Or it could even be the cutlery kit we mentioned earlier. The options are several – you can mix and match ideas, tailor them to the recipients' needs and preferences, and come up with an incredible gift in the process!

99.

Gift an experience or a skill

Why do gifts always need to be an object? You could give experiences or online subscriptions to classes or courses – like a calligraphy/madhubani art workshop, or something like pottery classes. You could offer your skill and time to them in a cool coupon or letter that they can use anytime in the year. The joy of gifting someone an experience of an activity that they have always wanted to do is unbeatable!

GIFTING IDEAS

1. HOMEMADE GOODIES

2. GENTLY-USED BOOKS, TOYS, ETC...

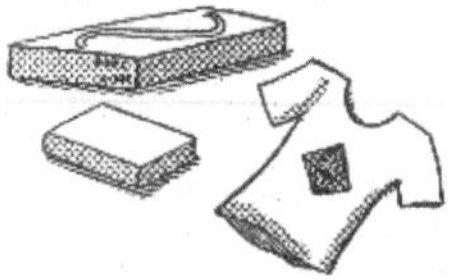

3. POTTED PLANTS

4. HANDMADE STUFF

5. GIFT EXPERIENCES

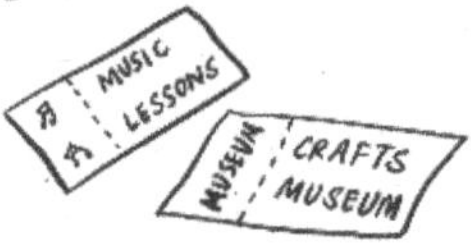

6. A DONATION

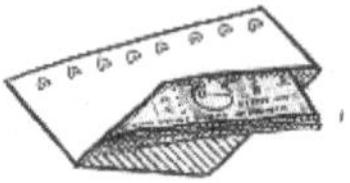

(TO A CAUSE THE RECIPIENT REALLY CARES ABOUT)

8

AGENT OF CHANGE

Visit a landfill or a dump yard near you

If you have never visited a landfill, this is your sign to do so! It can be a life-changing and eye-opening experience to actually see and understand the sheer scale of the problem we are facing today. Talk to the people who work there to understand the negative impact of unsegregated waste and leachate in human, animal and plant lives. Now, think about the journey of the waste you throw in the municipal dustbins. What can you do to reduce generating the waste in the first place?

100

'Recyclable' does not mean it will be recycled

The word 'recyclable' has to be one of the most misused and misunderstood words in the world of sustainable living. From coffee mugs to food packaging to takeaway food containers, 'recyclable' does not mean it will all be magically picked up and 100 per cent recycled. So, always choose the option where you are creating less waste in the first place. Use your own mugs and containers that can be washed and reused. And don't forget to spread the word about this.

101.

Where is your city's MRF?

MRF stands for material recovery facility. This is a facility where you can deposit your recyclable (dry) waste (even those that are refused by kabadiwalas) in a segregated manner. The MRF then sends it to waste processing and recycling facilities. So, make it a point to find out about your nearest MRF and plan out the disposal of the dry recyclable waste that you generate monthly at home.

102.

Write to your local elected representative

As a first step, get to know your councillors, MLAs and MPs. Find out and note down their social media handles, email IDs, phone numbers and office location/address. Writing to them about environmental concerns and problems consistently may yield positive results. The important thing here is to keep the communication and engagement constructive and alive.

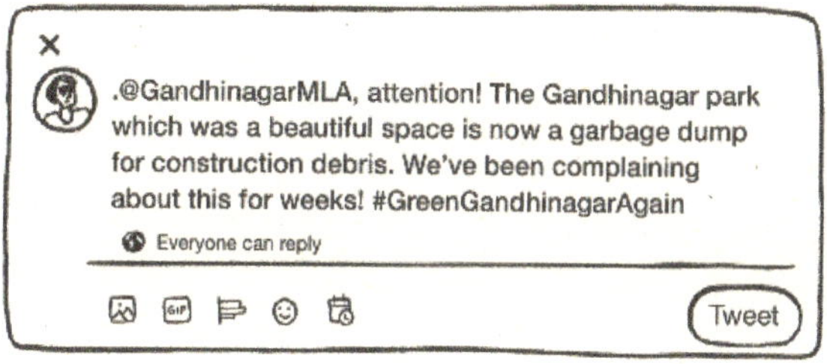

103.

Like. Share. Influence and change!

It does not matter how simple or small your act of thoughtfulness is.

Carrying a cloth bag for shopping? Take a photo and share it!

Using your own mug for takeaway coffee? Share it!

Carrying your own cutlery/straw during travel? Great! Click a pic and share your 'why'!

See others doing such things? Encourage, like and amplify!

Irrespective of our social media clout, we all can influence and inspire people and the local bodies through our conviction, practices and stories. What is important is to practice what we preach, share our journey – the successes, the failures, the attempts and the hacks – both online and offline.

104.

No voice or action is too small

Every time you shop somewhere or buy food at a restaurant, ask them for a reusable alternative to single-use items. Keep pushing and reminding them of the 'why'.

If you are part of a group (at your apartment/ fitness group/art group, etc.), share the 'why' behind your sustainable choices.

Teach children not to litter and to skip single-use plastic. Children internalize this important message and act as great amplifiers.

Nudge, don't preach. Regular, gentle nudges work better than lectures and admonishment.

105.

Support and amplify local green businesses

There are many local, small businesses that are making important efforts to bring zero-waste practices into their daily activities or switching to selling only responsible, ethically sourced and environmentally-friendly products with no plastic packaging. They may never be able to compete with big businesses. So, such small businesses need our support. Take the effort to get to know them, support them and amplify them via your network and social media channels.

106.

Support the waste-picking community

Waste pickers are a crucial part of the low-waste initiatives of any city. Sadly, they are often not recognized, appreciated or made an integral part of any program right from the planning stage. Work with your community to recognize and appreciate the effort of the local waste pickers, kabadiwalas and other sanitary workers that are employed in your neighbourhood. If there are small things you can do to improve the quality of their working environment, like providing drinking water facilities and a place for them to sit and rest, that will help.

107.

Go plogging, go!

Be it plogging (picking up trash while running) or organizing clean-ups, any such activity that brings the community together and raises awareness is much-needed in the long run. Even though we still need to raise awareness about reducing consumption and avoiding waste creation in the first place, it is promising to see more and more people engaging in clean-ups. It means that the awareness of the importance of a low-waste journey will go up. And people will see the reason to cut down on waste all the more clearly.

Instagram
plog-jog-log
♥1
plog_jog_log
Just another weekend run, jogging with friends and picking up trash at the Lake Gardens. Will be sharing the location of our next weekend's #plogrun soon join us? Bring your own reusable water bottle, and get ready to leave the place better than we found it!
#leavenotrace #plogging #loveyourplanet

108.

Change begins with you

As you educate yourself on sustainability and zero-waste living, these are a few terms you will come across. It's worth spending some time to learn what they mean.

Environmental racism	Environmental justice
Climate change	Climate justice
Fair Trade	Greenwashing
Ragpickers rights	EPR - extended producer responsibility
Permaculture	Circular economy and linear economy

Educating yourself and increasing your own awareness is the biggest, most important step in this journey towards a sustainable, zero-waste life.

109.

A simple mantra

Here's a quick list to mentally run through when you need something and plan to go buy it:

- Can you make do with what you already have?
- Can you borrow it from someone?
- Can you exchange or swap it with someone?
- Would that be available in a used or second-hand store? Example: last year's version of a mobile phone could be available at half the cost of the latest version
- Do you 'have to' buy it? Is that something you can DIY at home? Or you and your friends can make it yourself?

These questions are a good way to really rethink our purchases. Re-thinking consumption and buying only what we absolutely need is a good way to start our zero-waste journey.

110.

Planning. Progressing. Learning.

In this journey of low consumption, low-waste living, it is easy to get distracted by the many carefully curated social media posts on zero-waste/ sustainable living. Many of these posts and blogs may not show the actual reality or the long journey (or the paid promotions). We need to be realistic and mindful of our own challenges and struggles, given the context of our daily life, privileges, lack of a support system and so on. Hence, we need to be clear about our 'why', be kind to ourselves (and those we live with!) and take it one thing at a time in our quest for a sustainable, mindful, low-waste life.

Conclusion

Most of these tips are based on the practices, bits, and personal experiences of people who are passionate and practical about a zero-waste life in India. We had a tough time picking just 110 of those tips! There are countless zero-waste hacks and ideas – and in India, a lot of it comes to us intuitively because the concept of not wasting resources is not new to us. If we think back to how our grandparents lived, chances are, we will find at least a few practices we can adopt. If you want to share a tip or two with us which should've been in this book, let us know! We're on Instagram at @srini091 and @thehungrypalette.

While in this pursuit of sustainable living, it will serve us well to remember that everyone's journey may not look the same. Someone may be able to leapfrog and do waste segregation, start composting, and make bio enzymes within a month of starting on this path while someone may only be able to skip buying bottled water as a low-waste practice initially. Due to personal constraints and reasons beyond our locus of control, not everyone can adopt low/zero-waste practices right away. ***And that is okay!*** It is important to remember that we are on our way and are moving forward. Since the larger system is not really designed for or conducive to those who want to lead a simple, green, low-waste life, we must start with the easy wins first and then move on to the tougher battles.

We hope these tips help you as starting points to various lifelong habits or practices. Remember to explore and enjoy this journey of becoming an **eco-warrior**! Every bit counts!